UNDERSTANDINGSCIENCE

MOTION & MOVEMENT

PUBLISHED BY SMART APPLE MEDIA
1980 Lookout Drive, North Mankato, Minnesota 56003

Copyright © 2003 Smart Apple Media. International copyright reserved in all countries. No part of this book may be reproduced in any form without written permission from the publisher.

PHOTOGRAPHS by Gary Benson, Richard Cummins, David Davis, The Image Finders (Jim Baron, Mark E. Gibson, Dave Haas, Greg Hildebrandt, Michael Philip Manheim), Tom Myers Photography (Tom Myers, M. Nevins), NASA, Tom Stack & Associates (Erwin & Peggy Bauer, Mike Severns), Unicorn (Arni Katz, Mike Lepsch, Tom McCarthy, Daniel J. Olson, Herbert L. Stormont)

DESIGN AND PRODUCTION Evansday Design

LIBRARY OF CONGRESS CATALOGING-IN-PUBLICATION DATA

Frisch, Joy.
Motion and movement / by Joy Frisch.
p. cm. — (Understanding science)
Includes index.

Summary: Examines the topics of motion, force, gravity, and friction.

ISBN 1-58340-160-1

1. Motion—Juvenile literature. 2. Force and energy—Juvenile literature. [1. Motion. 2. Force and energy.] I. Title. II. Understanding science (North Mankato, Minn.).

QC133.5 .F75 2002

531'.11—dc21   2001054925

First Edition

9 8 7 6 5 4 3 2 1

Motion
&Movement

UNDERSTANDING SCIENCE

[Joy Frisch]

THE WORLD AROUND US IS ALWAYS IN MOTION. MOTION OCCURS WHENEVER SOMETHING CHANGES PLACE OR POSITION. PEOPLE WALK AND RUN. ANIMALS SWIM, FLY, LEAP, AND CRAWL. IN ORDER TO MAKE SOMETHING MOVE, A **FORCE** IS REQUIRED. PEOPLE AND ANIMALS HAVE MUSCLES THAT PRODUCE THE FORCE THEY NEED TO MOVE. MACHINES ARE POWERED BY ENGINES OR MOTORS. WITHOUT FORCES, NOTHING WOULD EVER HAPPEN.

A **force** is a pushing, pulling, or turning power that causes an object to move, stop, or change direction.

Forces can slow objects down, speed them up, or change their direction. There are pulling, pushing, and turning forces in action all around us. Any moving object has **kinetic energy**, or **energy** in motion. A snowball rolling down a mountain has a lot of kinetic energy. As it rolls faster and gets bigger, it gets more and more kinetic energy. **If an object is not too big, a person can use his or her muscles to exert the force required to move it. However, objects with greater mass require bigger forces. For instance, it is easy to pick up a box of cereal and move it, but much more force is required to move a piano.** Many machines, including big machines such as cars and small machines such as

Kinetic energy *is the energy possessed by an object that is moving.*

Energy *is the power or ability to do work.*

Mass *is the measure of the amount of material or matter that makes up an object.*

THE FORCE OF GRAVITY GIVES A DOWNHILL SKIER KINETIC ENERGY

Skiers often use wax to reduce the friction between the snow and their skis; this helps them travel faster. Swimmers wear caps and smooth swimsuits in order to reduce friction.

PEOPLE HAVE LONG USED GEARS TO MOVE POWER THROUGH MACHINES

clocks, operate through the use of **gears**. Gears move power from one part of a machine to another. They make parts move fast or slow. When muscle strength is not enough, special tools are sometimes used to move objects. A lever can be used to help lift or move heavy objects. A pulley, a wheel with a rope around it, is often used at building sites to lift heavy loads. Wheels and rollers also make movement easier. With wheels, an object can be rolled along easily instead of dragged.

Gears are two or more toothed wheels that fit together and cause each other to move.

With its sleek coat and slim body, the streamlined cheetah is the world's fastest land animal. Other wild cats are also built to move silently and swiftly, which aids them in hunting for food.

What goes up must come down. **Gravity** is the reason that objects fall to the earth. It is the force that pulls objects toward one another. Human muscle is a force capable of moving objects, but the force of gravity can be much stronger than muscle strength. All objects attract one another. The amount of their gravitational force depends on their mass. For instance, the earth has far more mass than an apple, so the gravitational pull of the earth is much stronger than the pull of the apple. The famous scientist Sir Isaac Newton discovered this idea more than 300 years ago when he saw an apple fall from a tree. Newton wondered how far the force of gravity reached into space. He realized that it might extend all the way to the moon, which would explain why the moon stays in **orbit** around the earth. It's

Gravity is a force that pulls objects downward toward the middle of the earth.

*An object in **orbit** travels in a curved path around another object.*

A PARACHUTE, IN EFFECT, REDUCES THE PULL OF GRAVITY ON A PERSON

If a balloon is blown up and then re-leased, it will fly around the room. This illustrates that for every action, there is an equal reaction. The air rushes out the end of the balloon, propelling the balloon in the other direction.

hard to imagine what life would be like without gravity. Walking would be impossible because our feet would not touch the floor. Things would not stay where we left them because they would float around the room like astronauts in outer space. The moon has enough gravity to hold astronauts onto its surface, but they have far less **weight** there than on Earth. Astronauts on the moon weigh only one-sixth of what they weigh on Earth, although their mass does not change. Earth's gravity pulls objects downward with a certain amount of force, which we call weight. The moon has much

The bottom of a bathtub can be very slippery, but a rubber bath mat creates more friction to give a better grip. Likewise, athletic shoes have rubber soles that give a person solid footing when running or playing sports.

Weight is the measurement of the gravitational force acting on an object.

EARTH'S GRAVITY IS STRONG ENOUGH TO KEEP THE MOON IN ITS ORBIT

less mass than the earth, so its gravity is much weaker. The gravitational force between the planets and the sun is great enough to hold them together in our solar system, even while they are moving through space. Like Earth, the sun has great mass and therefore has great gravitational pull. Gravity keeps everything in the universe in place, from people and houses to planets and stars.

If a person wants to move an object, he or she needs force. All objects will resist a force trying to move them. This resistance to movement is called **iner-tia**. The force needed to overcome inertia depends on the mass of the object. More massive objects have more inertia and therefore require more force to change their state of motion. An elephant has a lot more inertia, for example, than a pencil does. It is easy to move a pencil from its state of rest. It takes a lot more force to move an elephant. Inertia also keeps objects moving. All moving objects have inertia. They keep moving until another force stops them. Once launched into space, a spacecraft will continue to travel until a force acts upon it. A moving object will resist any force that might alter the speed at which it is going or change its direction. A

Inertia is an object's resistance to movement or to a change in motion.

INERTIA MUST BE OVERCOME BY A FORCE SUCH AS GRAVITY OR FRICTION

There are more than 600 muscles in the human body that pull on bones to make the body move. The contraction or extension of these muscles generates the force that puts the body in motion.

JETS FLYING FASTER THAN THE SPEED OF SOUND HAVE GREAT INERTIA

stone thrown across water, for example, will resist

sinking by skipping over the water. It continues

skipping until gravity stops its forward movement

and it sinks.

Rubbing your hands together to keep warm on a cold day is an example of friction. The surface of one hand rubbing against the surface of the other hand generates heat.

Whenever things touch, there is a force called **friction** that stops them from slipping. We may still slip sometimes on ice or other slippery surfaces, but most of the time friction gives us solid footing. If it were not for friction, the world would be a very strange place. Everything would keep sliding. A person couldn't ride a bike or even walk without friction. Friction is a force that slows down moving objects. Without it, moving objects would continue to move once they were set in motion. Friction occurs because no surface is perfectly smooth, however flat it may appear. Friction increases as the pressure between two surfaces increases. This is why heavier objects are harder to slide than light ones. Resistance to movement comes not only from the inertia of the object itself, but also from the surface over which it is traveling. A ball rolling across grass will soon slow down and stop because of the

Friction *is a force created when two objects rub together; it stops things from moving or slows them down.*

FRICTION KEEPS BALLS AND OTHER OBJECTS FROM ROLLING TOO FAR

We use the movement of air in many ways. Sailboats have large sails that catch the wind and use it to push them through the water. Windmills catch and use the power of wind to turn gears and generate energy.

resistance of the grass to the ball. The rougher the surface, the greater the force of friction. Sometimes friction is helpful, such as when a car needs to stop quickly to avoid a crash. The friction between the tires and the brakes of the car, as well as the friction between the tires and the road, will cause the car to stop. In addition to slowing down moving objects, friction also generates heat. Rubbing two sticks together and creating friction is an ancient way of making fire. In some situations, however, friction slows down objects that need to go fast, so people try to devise ways to minimize

A whole line of dominoes can be toppled when just one is knocked down. Kinetic energy is transferred from one domino to another until all the dominoes in the line have fallen over.

SINCE ITS INVENTION, THE WHEEL HAS SERVED A WIDE ARRAY OF USES

friction. The invention of the wheel made life much easier for ancient people, because wheels allowed them to travel faster and more easily than they could on foot. Carts also made it easier for people to pull heavy loads. With the invention of the wheel, friction was greatly reduced because the

A DOLPHIN'S SLEEK BODY KEEPS WATER'S DRAG TO A MINIMUM

surface area in contact with the ground was reduced. Friction resists movement over solid surfaces, but it also occurs when objects move through
liquids and gases. Friction on an object moving
through water or air causes **drag**, slowing the object down. Water produces more drag than air. Dol-
phins, sharks, and eagles are **streamlined** and
glide through water or air with ease. To reduce

drag, ships, submarines, and airplanes have shapes very similar to these animals. People who design machines to move through air or water want to keep drag forces as small as possible. The more slippery or streamlined a vehicle's shape, the faster or farther it will travel on a given amount of fuel. Racing cars have shiny, rounded surfaces that are shaped to reduce drag. A smooth, streamlined design cuts down on the amount of friction that occurs when the cars rub against air and helps the cars move very fast. Sometimes, though, drag is useful. For example, parachutists depend on the friction between the air and their parachutes to land softly and safely.

Drag *is the tendency for air or a liquid to slow a moving object.*

Streamlined *objects are shaped to minimize friction; water or air flows smoothly over moving streamlined objects.*

Ancient Greeks believed that when an arrow was shot into the air, it was the air itself that kept the arrow moving. The great Italian scientist Galileo Galilei later discovered that once an object was moving, no extra force was needed to keep it moving. He said that an object stops moving when another force, such as gravity, acts on it. The most famous scientist to study motion was Sir Isaac Newton, who took Galileo's ideas further. The **laws of motion** established by Newton describe how objects move when they are acted upon by forces. He said that a force makes an object move, and that it can also change how fast the object moves and the direction in which it is moving. Newton established three laws of motion. The first law states that if an object is not being pushed or pulled by a force, it will either stay still or keep moving in a straight line at a steady speed. This is also known

Laws of motion *are ideas that explain how objects move and react when they are acted upon by outside forces.*

MANY PEOPLE ENJOY THE GRAVITY-INDUCED PLUNGES OF ROLLER COASTERS

Inertia helps to keep roller coaster passengers in their seats as cars turn completely upside down. Gravity is the force that draws screams from passengers when the roller coaster zooms down sharp drops.

ALL THE LAWS OF MOTION ARE ILLUSTRATED DURING THE LAUNCH OF A SHUTTLE

as the law of inertia. Newton's second law states that when a force acts on an object, the object accelerates in the direction of the force. A force acting on a stationary object makes it start to move. A force acting on a moving object will speed it up, slow it down, or change its direction. The third law states that when an object is pushed or pulled, it will push or pull with equal strength in the opposite direction. Newton's laws of motion can be seen during the launch of a space shuttle. Before the engines fire, the shuttle sits still on a launch pad. This illustrates the first law: an object at rest will stay at rest until a force acts on it. When the engines fire, the shuttle lifts off. This illustrates the second law, which says that when a force acts on an object, the object changes its speed or direction in the same direction as the force that has been applied. The rocket lifts off because there is a tremendous force pushing it, which comes from the burning gas streaming backward from the engines. This illustrates Newton's third law, which says that

When pulling on an oar, a rower pushes water backward. This creates a force that moves the boat forward. The same thing happens when a person swims, kicking the water backward to move forward through the water.

JUMPING IS MADE POSSIBLE BY NEWTON'S THIRD LAW OF MOTION

for every force or action, there is an equal force or reaction against it. The third law is further illustrated by the motion of a person jumping on a trampoline. When a person jumps on a trampoline, he or she exerts a downward force on the trampoline. The trampoline then pushes the person back up into the air with an equal force or reaction. This illustrates that forces occur in pairs. The forces of motion can be great fun. Playgrounds use different types of force in a variety of ways. When we swing on a swing set, gravity is the force that pulls us downward again. Inertia keeps us from stopping at the bottom so we continue moving backward and forward. When we turn on a merry-go-round, we feel the **centrifugal force** pulling our bodies outward. On a slide, gravity does all the work, pulling us downward along the slope. Forces of motion cannot be seen, but we experience their effects all the time. They keep our feet on the ground and hold everything on Earth in place. Everywhere around us, gravity and other forces of movement are constantly at work. By learning more about Newton's laws of motion, we can better understand the movement of the world around us.

*A **centrifugal force** is a force that pulls a spinning object outward.*

THE FASTER AN OBJECT MOVES, THE GREATER THE FORCE NEEDED TO STOP IT

Inertia is the tendency for an object in motion to stay in motion, or an object at rest to stay at rest. This experiment will let you and a friend see and feel inertia directly.

WHAT YOU NEED
Masking tape
A pen

WHAT YOU DO

1. Put a piece of masking tape on the sidewalk and label it point A.

2. Starting at point A, take 20 long steps. Put down another piece of masking tape and label it point B.

3. Beginning at point A, run as fast as you can to point B. Try to stop exactly on the tape at point B *without slowing down ahead of time.*

4. Now, watch as your friend repeats step 3. Was either of you able to stop exactly on the tape?

WHAT YOU SEE
Because of inertia, your body—put in motion by the force of your muscles—continues in a straight line at the same speed. Your moving body builds up momentum, or forward movement. To stop momentum, a moving object either needs to slow down ahead of time or crash into another object of greater mass. That is the reason you can't stop abruptly on the line after running at full speed, no matter how hard you try. Your body keeps going instead.

INDEX